Raising Kings

Book of Poems

by
Sharika K. Forde
with Jaquan Forde

Watersprings
PUBLISHING

Raising Kings: Book of Poems
published by Watersprings Publishing,
a division of Watersprings Media House, LLC.
P.O. Box 1284 Olive Branch, MS 38654
www.waterspringsmedia.com

Contact the publisher for bulk orders and permission requests.

Printed in the United States of America.

ISBN-13: 979-8-9859594-5-1

Table of Contents

CHAPTER 1: SLAVE EFFECTS 1
   Move On 2
   The Infiltration of the Black Man. 3
   What Do You See? 4
   Trust in Us 5
   Slave Effects 6
   George Floyd....What If?. 8
   Last Name X 9

CHAPTER 2: THE CONCRETE JUNGLE 10
   Fear of the Black Man 11
   Envy 12
   Dangerous Animals. 13
   The Concrete Jungle 14
   Justice for All 15
   A Village Dismantled. 16
   Cold World Warm Heart. 17

CHAPTER 3: WE RISE 18
   From Fields to Streets 19
   Go Back to Africa! 20
   See Me 21
   We Rise 22
   Above All Else. 23
   Fear to Freedom 24
   Years in the Making 25
   King Mentality 26
   A Star is Born. 27
   Wear your Crown with Pride 28
   The Black Man's Fight. 29

CHAPTER 4: REINTRODUCING MY SON 30
    The Conversation 32
    Putting You on Game 33
    Melanin Gold 34
    Respect Your Queen 35
    This or That 36
    One Dribble at a Time 37
    A Day in The Life 38
    Where I aim to be 39
    Patriarch 40
    Mother Dearest 41

CHAPTER 5: AS A CHILD 42
    Two Crowns 43
    The Me You Cannot See 44
    I Am My Father's Child 46
    A Mother's Love 47
    Protect Our Young Kings 48
    Birth of Jaciah 49

ABOUT THE AUTHOR 51

This book is dedicated to all black men.

Men that we've loved.

Men that we've lost.

Fathers, Brothers, Uncles, Sons.

We watched your struggle.

We heard your cry.

We felt your pain.

Throughout it all you have flourished.

You are a King!

Chapter 1

Slave Effects

Move On

They tell us to move on
From the days we were enslaved
And held in chains

Forbidden to speak out of turn
Or look straight in the eyes of a pale face

The Texas border
got men on horses
Targeted while grocery shopping
No knock warrants

Am I to accept
the racial inequality
In this country
For people who look like me

How can I move on
When racism
is staring
me in the face.

The Infiltration of the Black Man

Strapped to ships and stolen away
Shackled to keep him in place
Hunted when he escaped to find peace
Whipped when he didn't bow to their feet
Hung when he refused a lifetime of pain
The infiltration of the black man
Under attack since he took his first breath.

What Do You See?

What do you see when you see me
Kaep silently took a knee
A prodigy on the field
Yet told not to think

You saw disrespect to your country
Black folks dawned camouflage
Lost their lives, shed blood
Fighting for a place where we are still
Fighting for equality

When you see what you wanna see
You will never see me.

Trust in Us

Dark vs. Light
Strong vs. Weak
Whether picking cotton
Or serving in the big house
We were still property.

Taught to judge and criticize
We break the dreams of others
Who look just like Us
All because we were brainwashed
To not trust in Us.

Slave Effects

Decades later
the effects of slavery
still haunts you.

Fighting to get to the top
of a mountain that seems
impossible to climb.

Taking two steps forward
then falling four steps behind.

It's hard to shine
when slave effects
stand still in time.

i watched the video
and i knew
what i was about to see
my mind still didn't comprehend
a modern day lynching in 2020
and the murderer didn't even blink
witnesses screaming for him to move his knee
the murderer pressed harder
he cried "MAMA"
and took his last breath.

George Floyd....What If?

What if there were no video?
Would you have believed the crowd?
Screaming voices echoed throughout the hood

What if there were no video?
Would you have believed the police?
Who said he was fighting back
While bearing his knee on his neck
Screaming "MAMA' over and over again

The world watched George Floyd
Take his last breath
Just for being black.

Last Name X

Our names were stolen from us.
Carried by ship whether forced or tricked
They made us feel pain
Stripped us of our names
Mind games to erase from where we came
Erased our heritage, tribe and identity
Labeled us with the last name of our "master"
Still carrying their potent legacy
As we gained freedom
We gained knowledge of self
Dropped that slave name for one letter
Last Name X

Chapter 2

The Concrete Jungle

Fear of the Black Man

When you are unarmed
You are still armed

Due to your strength
They fear you

Try to control your mind
They imprison you

Keep you in debt
They don't promote you

Can't feed your babies

So, you do what you gotta do.

Envy

They want to murder you
Because you won't let your melanin stop you
Jealousy and greed filling the hole
Where love has been voided
And no longer grows

Watch the company you keep
Applaud in your face
When your back is turned
A hissing sound can be heard
Envy is an incredible beast.

Dangerous Animals

The system wants us to hate each other
Broadcast criminal activity
Across all channels
Label us as dangerous animals
Reject our pain
Reject our mental strife
Lock us behind bars
Bail set at a high price
Trapped in a cage
Criminal record stamped by our name
Bait us together
They sit back
Watch us become each other's prey.

The Concrete Jungle

Feeling the world
On your shoulders
While swimming
Under water
With no
Life preserver
Redlines blocking your escape
From the concrete jungle.

Justice for All

Justice for one
Should equal justice for all
But we don't stand a chance
When our skin is dark
And are hair is coiled

Another black man dead
Lying on the ground
Bullets in the back of his head
Trigger pulled by the men in blue
Claiming self defense

No justice, no peace
Repeated so long
You can hear the tone
Without mouthing the words

Still the message falls
Empty ears for those
Who never experience
The cruelty of this world
When will there be
Justice for All.

A Village Dismantled

It's not our village, it's theirs
The deed belongs to them
A village dismantled.
The war on drugs
Created a one on one battle.
Out here fighting each other
With no camouflage.
Our pain is public
But some say it's a mirage.

We went from
Being broke
To looking for hope
To staying woke.

Our bodies are bonded.
African blood burns
Through our veins
Unimaginable strength.

The village is dismantled
Burn it down
We building mansions instead.

Cold World Warm Heart

At times you get so angry
Want to rip the world apart.
Still I see the glow in your heart.
Hold on to the hurt
The other side of pain is love.
It lives in abundance

This cold world tells you
You are not good enough
You are not smart enough
Your strength is diminished
by the weakness within.

Reject every negative image
They try to plant inside of you
Whatever this cold world
Throws at you
Throw it back
With a message from your ancestors.
No matter what you go through
You will overcome.
Hold your head high
Straighten your crown
Stand proud in your blackness.
Don't let this cold world
Break your warm heart.

Chapter 3

We Rise

From Fields to Streets

Since the days held hostage on plantations
To live or die was the only decision
From fields to streets
Survival mode
From leaders in the Motherland
To claiming corners we don't own
Where many Kings die young
We traded the fields for streets

Go Back to Africa!

Caged us, enslaved us.
Made us build your haven.
Raped us cause our curves
Had you craving
Sold our babies off the plantation
Hung us cause we were "misbehaving"
Now we have higher education
Stand up for our rights in our nation
Kneeled in protest of the system
Turned red states blue
Changing the narration
Owning businesses
Setting the foundation
Raisings Kings and Queens
Uniting generations
All while you still screaming
Go back to Africa

See Me

You don't see color
But I want you to see my blackness
The depth of my roots
The pride in my heritage.
The generations of courage
So I can look you straight in your eyes
While I hold my fist high and scream
I'm black and I'm proud

We Rise

You question the existence
Of our resistance
But refuse to
Acknowledge our presence
We rise above the prejudice
The racist comments
The police harassment
Your unfair practices
We remove the distractions
Stand by our actions
Live for our passions
We Rise.

Above All Else

We close our eyes
Dreaming of a better life
Born with the ability to rise
Above all else.

Our struggles
Our strengths
Our stories

All pieces of us
Place it all together
And rise above all else.

Fear to Freedom

Fear of
Success
Failure
Self
Fear makes us stronger
Work harder
More prepared
Take the fear
And turn it into
Freedom.

Years in the Making

Black Businesses
Black Bosses
Black Entrepreneurs
The movement has been years in the making
Black Power
Black Pride
Black Excellence
The movement has been years in the making
Black Mothers
Black Fathers
Black Unification
The movement has been years in the making
Black Love
Black Support
Black Everything
The movement has been years in the making.

King Mentality

You are more than a man
You are a King
Your strength
Your pride
Your courage
And fearless loyalty
Your wisdom
Your heart
And your giving ways
You protect
You provide
And your love runs deep
You are the embodiment
of all things royal
This is the essence of a
King's mentality.

A Star is Born

Everyday a star is born
And that includes you
Created in his image
There are no mistakes
For each feature
is perfectly placed

wide nose
coiled hair
broad shoulders
opulent lips
shining melanin

But it's your remarkable mind
Unparalleled to others
The King inside of you
Is waiting to shine
Don't hold back
Show the world who you are
A Star.

Wear your Crown with Pride

Sometimes our crowns get heavy
and we question ourselves

Double guessing
our decisions and paths for our lives

The outside looks confident
While inside is full of confusion
Wondering if our dreams are really a delusion

Continue to dream big and wear your crown with pride.

We are Kings and Queens

It's in our bloodline.

The Black Man's Fight

Raised by my father
Minded by my brothers
Witnessing
The Black Man's fight
Watching the world
In a different light
Confidence brewing
As a determined woman
Using my words
To speak power
To an unheard community

The Black Man's Fight
The fight for family
The fight for justice
The fight for equality

Fist Clutched.
Head Bowed.
Standing Proud.

Chapter 4

Reintroducing My Son

Queens and Kings
aren't just raised in the home.
My son, who has fathered none.
But raising leaders in his role
as a school counselor and coach
also has the gift of flow.
He is sharing his soul
in the following poems.

Reintroducing my son,
King Jaquan Forde

The Conversation

A kid asks me how do you forgive when u want to kill
And I knew the pain behind the question was real
Squeeze my feet in his shoes I'd express how he feels
But as a mentor I must realize adversity builds
Guidance is passed with or without knowledge
Youths minds sit in our palms as we polish
Not everyone is meant for a four year college
But every melanin seed has a goal to accomplish

Every rock is crafted by its environment
Negative energy is normalized unless corrected
Picked up, tossed around without consent
Mudded blankets make it easy to be rejected
No explanation for trauma builds resent
Violence, fear tools used to be respected
Traditional trauma without acknowledgement
Leaves our youth subconsciously affected

I advised he recall his old friend's weathering
Common trauma induced bonds that let him in
Broken promises, permanent pain shared by friends
Make room for forgiveness, the hurtful cycle may end

Putting You on Game

I get it, I am not your father
Guidance is not something you desire
But for slum detachment, knowledge is required
You won't get most my gems until you are old
But even if unappreciated my goal is to mold
Short term glitter hardly turns gold
It's hard to see the end zone when your visor isn't clear
Neighborhood elders lost in failure and despair
Unhealthy cycles are meant to be dismantled
Toxic ideology cannot continue to ramble
Uplift melanin potential from the ground trampled
As Tupac said, after every dark night there's a brighter day
You are my future, I have no choice but to pave a way

Melanin Gold

What impact do you have on your youth?
We expect them to build without proper tools
Spitting image of me run halls of school
But instead of being like me I want them to improve

Find passion in extending helping hands
Uplifting guidance is in high demand
A village is required to raise a man
Planned Parenthood trips are never planned

No seeds in my garden but I help flowers grow
They look at me as authority, then big bro
No artistic bone, but I perfected my mold
Into beautiful nuggets of melanin gold

Respect Your Queen

We're born with a throne fitted king
Never fathom the responsibility it brings
It comes years before you buy the ring
That eighth grader seated two desk down from you
Was blessed with the same deep grounded roots
But our apples tumbled without well rounded tools
Money over "hoes", unhealthy goals, rotten our soil
Redirected anger, our queens feel the sour recoil
Compiled years of misuse, impossible to feel royal
Generational curses overlap, unconscious habits arrive
Media glorification fogs vision, leaving us deprived
Only a few black households stayed aligned

The malignant potion can be undone
Once our community unites, becomes one
And we fertilize the mud our seeds are from
We look at our sunflowers as delicate, frail
Put them in our shadows, not given their own trail
Yet our queens blossom, stems reaching for the grail
Just acknowledging beauty is an injustice to our flowers
Uplift the culture soaked in their roots, endorse her power
Not embracing their bright petals
are only signs of a coward
The black woman is a poetic renaissance,
not a flower to keep
Sister, mother, aunt, that girl two desk down,
are all Queens

This or That

You can raise a son or a gun
Swing a bat or sling some crack
Buy a Henny bottle or pampers for your toddler
Settle for life on "the streets" or extend your reach
Uplift troubled brothers or help put them under covers
Continuously frogger pass class or
pursue grants for UMass
Abuse lean as seen on TV or pursue a degree
Engage our sisters like meat or
plateau their pedestals like Queens
Be unwillingly buried 6 feet deep
or fertilize melanin trees

One Dribble at a Time

This 90 feet is your safe place
Your talking piece is the ball
Elders are your coaches, each adverse in skill
Defenders are the talking topics
The one right in front of you is doubt
Jab at the ambiguity
Once it's gone, side step past fears
Feeling overwhelmed? Step back and reset
Drive through the lane of opportunity
When obstacles pile up, kick out to teammates
Your corner is your backbone, make sure to assist
Emotionally confused? Take a timeout
Transitions become easy in life
Once you defend your peace
Euro step past distractions
Pivot and spin around adversity
Pump fake the haters,
but never hesitate when shooting your shot
Finally when life gives you free throws,
block the noise

A Day in The Life

Wake up to no toothpaste, clean socks or hair grease
Marked late on attendance
cuz I ain't want my Airs creased
I fell asleep first period, thanks mom for no curfew
Wake up in the middle of class, lost and confused
Lunch is my favorite period, today's Salisbury steak
Make sure to get seconds,
won't be much on my dinner plate
Gym class used to always be fun
But puberty hit, I was told I stunk!
Come winter I'm always sick,
hand me down fleece isn't thick
Even teachers have trouble talking to the kid
doused in Vicks

Where extra pencils used to stay, now lies gel and brushes
Force fields for his kicks since they're so precious
Cot and pillow hogs the corner, remedy for all-nighters
When I don't understand the lesson,
I go to the schoology sliders
Sometimes lunch isn't good, or bitesize, not enough
But I can always count on Ms. Peace snacks to fill me up
Stopped participating in gym,
saves me from next class jokes
But Pandolfo got me everything I need
when my sweat has me soaked
I saved up money to get a nice winter jacket
But Mr. Forde got me one, now I can get shoes to match it

Where I aim to be

Cul de sacs missing sidewalks
Bounty blankets atop marble countertops
Driveways covered in hopscotch chalk
Fridges saturated with edible colors
Tempurpedics I don't have to share with my brother
Fairytale endings with my high school lover
Opulent D1 dreams obtainable outside sleep
Dedicated trust funds keep my silver spoon sleek
Drums and bass, my only taste of the slum's mystique
8-year tuition, intellectual goals, lawyer, physician
One and done goals were second to true ambitions
Bird feed, completed ancestry tree, is where I aim to be

Patriarch

Every out of state ride came with gems
Combatted shelterness with a view from your lens
Curated our strength, brotherhood, confidence within
Hugs are seldom, but the love is everlasting
I regret the time not spent with each day passing
Your the reason my life's seat belt stays fasten
No sentence you utter is ever a waste of breath
Spoon fed wisdom even when we didn't want to digest
Family is everything, cherish Bajan blood and flesh

At the age of nine you took the heaviest steps
Underneath shaking was my world into new depths
Whirlwinds of emotions, but for the family it was best
A family with no King, how I perceived we'd live
Broken melanated homes
Misguided testosterone
All that was portrayed by my fatherless friends
But fatherhood bares no address, our odyssey didn't end
Car parts, Mark Sanchez starts,
all the needed lucrative lessons
July 20th, 1969
God granted my siblings and I
one of our biggest blessings.

Mother Dearest

Your warm love flourished through my childhood
It takes a man to raise one,
but without you I'd still be a boy
Sacrificing your happiness for our experience of joy
God blessed me with a black Queen in '94
Taught me love and respect heritage and culture
Your faith in me drives my motivation to go further
I hope to be a spitting image of your spirit when I'm older
Whether Survivor, The Office, even America's Top Model
Those laughs and jaw dropping scenes
helped our bond throttle
Kept all our hearts and spirits full in a world cold and hollow
Poetic justice does not fully describe your impact
So this art I inscribe,
expresses the love my actions may lack
I wear your hoodies and shirts with enormous pride
Layering books with raw emotions pouring from inside
Showing the gifts we could give with devoted time
From three-day ninety degree Hartford jazz heat
To Everything Sauce and vibes in Springfield streets
Even watching parachutes dive out East Hamden Fleets
Helping you gift your art to the world
Created memories glued to my core
When asked my favorite author
I proudly say Sharika K. Forde

Chapter 5

As a Child

Two Crowns

Two crowns form together in unification
To build a stronger foundation
A deep love, passion for life
No competition
Each wanting to see the other succeed
The beginning of the narration
An eternal destination
To be one.

The Me You Cannot See

The me you cannot see
is mixed in my DNA.
In an African village
thousands of miles away.
From the brick buildings in Jersey
that stood tall above me.
To the sun quenching my melanin
in the Florida rays.
Through my struggles in love.
Through my victories in life.
It's all pieces of my DNA
that makes me who I am today.
It's the me you cannot see.
I am a Queen, Raising Kings.

As a child, I watched.
I watched my father get up early every day to get myself and my brother ready for school. Then, off to work, then back home to housework. We had clean clothes, a roof over our heads and he ensured that we were well fed. My father was a single dad.

As a child, I listened.

I listened when my father talked about home ownership and investment properties. He talked about faith and although he strayed from the church, he found his way back eventually. He talked about family. He was the only one living up north, so his southern roots run deep.

When you observe a person for so long, the core of them finds its way to you. He wore his invisible crown high and with pride.

Myself, a single mother of four sons, I raise my children with the same greatness my father instilled in me. I encourage them to see beyond their dreams and turn their gifts into reality.

I Am My Father's Child

Distant relatives say
"Hey that's Jackie's daughter".
I reply back with a smile.
Proud that with just one look
They see your resemblance in me.

Daddy born in the 40's
Raised in the south.
He witnessed scenes of injustice
I've only seen on tv
But feel just as deep.

When I do speak
It's through your words.

As a little girl
I watched your every move.
I am you in the female form.
A bona fide daddy's girl.
I am my father's child.

A Mother's Love

They said I spoiled you
I did
What else is a mother to do?

Lord knows this world can be cold
So when you are in our home
It's nothing but love

Show you who you are
Before the world tries to tear you down

You are my seed
A leader and phenomenal being
Don't ever let anyone tell you less
You are a King

Protect Our Young Kings

Because of the streets
Because of the police
I always worry
So when you say "Ma, chill I'm good"
That sounds impossible to me
I need to hear your voice
I need to see your face
I pray every night
That you return home safe
God, protect our young Kings.

Birth of Jaciah

A push, short cry
Then you appeared
In silence, I wiped my tears
Brown eyes, thin curly hair
A smile so precious
It lifted my fears

The birth of Jaciah
My first grandchild. A male.
The world will watch you soar
The legacy continues
Another King is born.

ABOUT THE AUTHOR

Author Sharika K. Forde has a passion for creative expression. In 2017, she pushed her fear aside and published her first poetry book. She has since published a memoir, three poetry books, and a collection of children's books, all inspired by life lessons. Beginning each day with a prayer for good health, monetary wealth, and true love, she strives to live a life of fulfillment through her passion for writing.

Other Books by Sharika K.Forde

Poetry Books:
The Awakening Poems Vol 1; Bare Emotions of Love, Growth, & Self-Worth
The Awakening Poems Vol 2; I Dream in Color

Children's Books:
Grandma's Lil' King
Grandpa's Lil' Queen
Grandma's Lil' King Plays T-Ball
Grandma's Lil' Math King
The Moon, The Stars, and Fast Cars

Memoir:
From Brick Buildings to Beaches

Coloring Book:
Jaciah & Jayla's Zoo Adventure

linktr.ee/sharika_theauthor